FOCUS ON
THE USA

Christopher Hunt

Evans Brothers Limited

Published by Evans Brothers Limited
2A Portman Mansions
Chiltern Street
London W1M 1LE

© Evans Brothers Limited 1995

First published 1995

Design by TJ Graphics
Map by Jillie Luff, Bitmap Graphics
Editor Su Swallow
Production Jenny Mulvanny

Printed in Hong Kong by Dah Hua Printing Co. Ltd

ISBN 0 237 51438 9

Acknowledgements
The author and publishers would like to thank the following for permission to reproduce the photographs:
Zefa title page, 9 (left), 11 (right); Travel Photo International contents page, 11 (left), 18 (left); Ecoscene 4 (top), 10, 13 (left), 26 (bottom left), 27 (left); Robert Harding Picture Library 4 (bottom), 9 (right), 17 (right), 20 (right), 23 (right), 26 (top left, right), 28 (right), 29 (left), 31 (left); Bruce Coleman Limited 6, 7, 11 (centre left, bottom left), 15 (left), 16, 17 (left), 19 (left), 20 (left), 22; 24, 25, 28 (left); Hutchinson Library 13 (right), 30; Spectrum Colour Library 14, 19 (right), 21, Trip 29 (right), 31 (right)

Cover About two million people visit Mount Rushmore each year. Here the heads of four famous American presidents have been carved into the northeast side of the mountain. From left to right they are George Washington, Thomas Jefferson, Theodore Roosevelt and Abraham Lincoln. Each sculpture is about 20 metres high. The Mount Rushmore memorial celebrates America's founding, political philosophy, preservation and expansion. Work began on the project in 1927 and was completed in 1941.

Title page New York: the Statue of Liberty and the Manhattan skyline.

Opposite Navajo Indian land in Monument Valley, Arizona.

Contents

Introducing the USA

The United States of America is the fourth largest country in the world and has a population of almost 250 million. The USA has not always been as large as it is today. When it declared its independence from Great Britain on the 4th July, 1776 it consisted of just 13 states located along the eastern coast of North America. Today there are 50 states; 48 of these lie in North America between Canada and Mexico. The two newest states, Alaska and Hawaii, are separated from the rest of the country. (Alaska is northwest of Canada and Hawaii is a group of islands in the Pacific Ocean.)

The USA is a democracy. This means that the government is elected by the people. The United States was also the first country in the world to have a written constitution. The American Constitution describes how the country should be governed and the rights of the people living in the United States. The government is divided into three sections. Congress is responsible for making laws, the Supreme Court for interpreting the laws when disputes arise and the President appoints people to run the government and decides on policy towards other countries.

The USA has a great variety of landscape and climate. Temperatures range from the warmth of sub-tropical Florida (see page 11) where they exceed 30° C in the summer to the cold polar climate of Alaska (see page 6) where they may fall below -40° C in the winter. Generally, the east coast experiences milder conditions than the west, but the greatest extremes of temperature are found in the continental interior which can be very hot in summer and bitterly cold in winter.

Snow lingers on the highest mountains in the Rockies, Colorado, even in summer.

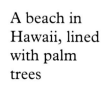

A beach in Hawaii, lined with palm trees

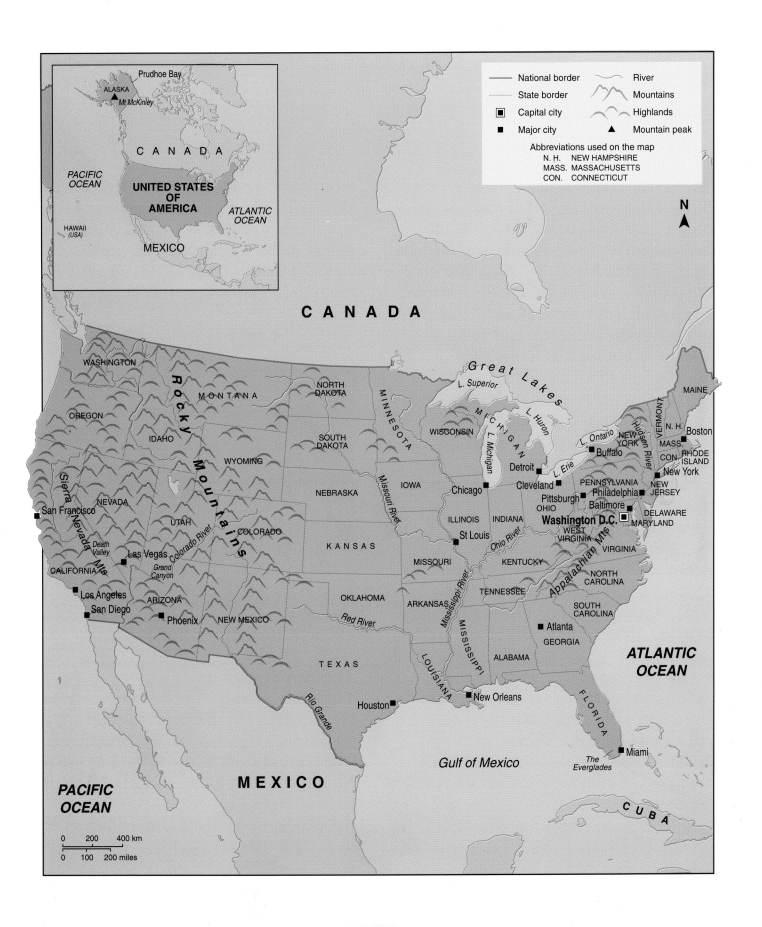

Legend

—— National border	River
—— State border	Mountains
☐ Capital city	Highlands
■ Major city	▲ Mountain peak

Abbreviations used on the map
N. H.   NEW HAMPSHIRE
MASS. MASSACHUSETTS
CON.   CONNECTICUT

N

CANADA

UNITED STATES OF AMERICA

PACIFIC OCEAN

HAWAII (USA)

MEXICO

ATLANTIC OCEAN

Prudhoe Bay

ALASKA

▲ Mt McKinley

CANADA

WASHINGTON

OREGON

IDAHO

MONTANA

NORTH DAKOTA

SOUTH DAKOTA

WYOMING

Rocky Mountains

Sierra Nevada Mts

NEVADA

UTAH

COLORADO

NEBRASKA

MINNESOTA

WISCONSIN

Great Lakes

L. Superior

L. Huron

MICHIGAN

L. Michigan

Death Valley

Las Vegas

Colorado River

Grand Canyon

CALIFORNIA

San Francisco

Los Angeles

San Diego

ARIZONA

Phoenix

NEW MEXICO

Red River

IOWA

Chicago

ILLINOIS

INDIANA

KANSAS

MISSOURI

St Louis

Ohio River

KENTUCKY

TENNESSEE

OKLAHOMA

ARKANSAS

Mississippi River

TEXAS

Houston

Rio Grande

LOUISIANA

New Orleans

MISSISSIPPI

ALABAMA

Detroit

Cleveland

L. Erie

L. Ontario

Buffalo

Pittsburgh

OHIO

PENNSYLVANIA

Philadelphia

Baltimore

Washington D.C. ☐

WEST VIRGINIA

MARYLAND

DELAWARE

NEW JERSEY

New York

VERMONT

N. H.

MAINE

Boston

MASS.

CON.

RHODE ISLAND

Hudson River

NEW YORK

VIRGINIA

Appalachian Mts

NORTH CAROLINA

SOUTH CAROLINA

Atlanta

GEORGIA

FLORIDA

The Everglades

Miami

ATLANTIC OCEAN

Gulf of Mexico

MEXICO

PACIFIC OCEAN

CUBA

| 0 | 200 | 400 km |
| 0 | 100 | 200 miles |

Mountains

The western mountain ranges

Much of the western half of the USA is occupied by high ranges of mountains. They extend from Alaska through Canada and the United States and then into Mexico. This area of mountains is almost 1500 kilometres wide in places, stretching from the Great Plains to the Pacific coastline. The Rockies (see page 4) are the highest range of mountains.

These mountains are largely made up of sedimentary rocks which have been pushed upwards by intense earth movements. Mountains formed in this way are called fold mountains. Some of the mountains are volcanoes or have been formed from flows of hot liquid rock called lava. Even today this region suffers earthquakes and volcanic eruptions.

The highest peaks occur in Alaska, where Mount McKinley rises 6194 metres above sea level. Spectacular scenery is common throughout the western mountain ranges. This is especially true of the Rockies, where rivers and glaciers have carved deep valleys through the mountains.

These mountains are not heavily populated because either they are too rugged or the climate is too dry or cold. The traditional occupations of people living in these mountains are ranching, lumbering or mining. Few major cities have developed here because the mountains are too remote to support most industries. But tourism is becoming increasingly important. In the summer people come to visit national parks and view the natural features. In winter they visit mountain resorts to enjoy the skiing.

Mount McKinley, the highest point in the USA

The Appalachians

The Appalachian mountains extend from New England in the north to Alabama in the south, a distance of 1900 kilometres. The highest peak in the Appalachians is Mount Mitchell in North Carolina which is 2037 metres above sea level. The Appalachians were once much higher than they are today but the rocks have been eroded (worn away), mainly by rivers.

Volcanoes

The largest and most active group of volcanoes in the USA is found in the Hawaiian Islands in the Pacific. These islands are merely the summits of a series of huge underwater volcanoes. Two volcanoes, Mauna Loa and Kilauea, are still active. The summit of Mauna Loa is 4170 metres above sea level but the island is 9150 metres above the sea bed. This makes it the largest active volcano in the world. Mauna Loa erupts on average every four years, releasing streams of very hot lava which can flow over 30 kilometres before it cools. Lava fountains sometimes spurt up to 15 metres high from cracks on the slopes of the volcano. These are known as curtains of fire. The lava can flow at speeds up to 40 km/h and will destroy anything in its path.

Active volcanoes also occur in the Cascades in the state of Washington. These volcanoes erupt far less frequently but with much greater explosive force.

National parks

National parks are large areas of land where the landscape is so beautiful or unusual that the government has decided to protect it. The parks are run by the National Park Service which provides facilities for visitors such as camp sites, nature trails and information centres. Most parks include large wilderness areas which are not accessible to the general public. This allows wildlife to remain undisturbed.

A volcano erupting in Hawaii

A beaver dam in the Teton National Park, Wyoming

The power of nature

The USA is such a large country that when natural events such as earthquakes, hurricanes and tornadoes occur in isolated areas they cause little interest. But sometimes they strike densely populated areas and thousands of people are faced with disaster.

Earthquakes

Earthquakes result from the sudden movement of huge sections of the Earth's crust called plates. This releases huge amounts of energy in the form of a shockwave or tremor. Most earthquakes occur close to the boundary between two plates.

The San Andreas faultline in California is the most active earthquake zone in the United States. It lies along the boundary of the Pacific Plate and the North American Plate. Each year it causes hundreds of small tremors to occur in the region. As a result, many buildings in California have been specially designed to withstand earthquakes. They have flexible foundations which should cause them to sway rather than collapse during a tremor. Children in Californian schools have regular drills so that they know how to protect themselves during an earthquake.

In January 1994, Los Angeles was declared a disaster area when an earthquake struck the San Fernando Valley, northwest of the city. It was the worst earthquake in southern California for 40 years. More than 50 people were killed, hundreds were injured, highways were destroyed, thousand of homes were wrecked and hundreds of fires sparked, leaving the city covered in thick, black smoke. The quake was unusually destructive because its epicentre was in a densely populated area.

Earthquakes are also common in Alaska. One of the strongest earthquakes ever recorded devastated the port of Valdez in 1964. It caused huge cracks in roads and buckled railway lines. Airport runways and bridges had to undergo major repairs. Tidal waves nine metres high, and massive landslides added to the devastation.

A freeway in California, after an earthquake

Hurricanes

Hurricanes are tropical storms that form over warm seas in the late summer or early autumn. The centre of the storm is called the eye and powerful winds blow around it at speeds of more than 160km/h. Hurricanes are likely to batter at least one part of the coastline of Florida or the Gulf of Mexico almost every year. They can even damage reinforced houses.

Fortunately it is possible to track the paths of hurricanes using satellites. This means that people can be warned about an approaching hurricane and evacuate towns and cities in its path. But they may return to find their homes wrecked by either the wind or floods.

Tornadoes

Tornadoes, or twisters, are the most powerful winds that form over land. They are spiralling funnels of wind, rarely more than a few hundred metres wide but rotating at great speed, often more than 400 km/h. They are most likely to form in wet conditions during the summer on the Great Plains. Their paths are difficult to predict but anything in their way is almost certain to be picked up and destroyed. Tornadoes have been responsible for the deaths of more than 9000 people in the USA since 1930.

Hurricane damage in Florida

The storm of the century

In March 1993, the greatest storm this century struck 25 eastern and southern states. It created strong winds in excess of 160 km/h. In some southern states more snow fell in 24 hours than normally falls in a year. In Florida the storm triggered around 50 tornadoes. Waves 10 metres high battered the coastline and at least 115 people were killed by the storm.

A tornado sweeps across Nebraska.

Natural environments

Forests

The USA has vast areas of forests and woodlands. But it is estimated that about half of the original area of natural forests has either been cut down for timber or cleared for farmland. In recent years much more thought has been given to the conservation of forests but many places remain under threat from developers as well as from pollution and acid rain.

In the west, wetter mountain areas such as the Rockies are covered with forests of evergreen trees such as pine, spruce and fir. In the east there are also extensive areas of forest and woodland in the southern Appalachians. These forests contain more than 140 varieties of trees including hickory, poplar, walnut and sycamore. Sub-tropical plants such as magnolias, laburnums and rhododendrons are also able to grow here because of the warm temperatures.

These redwoods, called Giant Sequoia, are between 2000 and 3000 years old.

The most spectacular trees are the redwoods that grow along the north coast of California. The warm damp climate of this region has enabled these to become the tallest trees in the world. The tallest redwood on record is 112 metres high – more than twice the height of Nelson's Column in London.

Deserts

An estimated 1,500,000 square kilometres of the USA can be classified as desert. The deserts are found in the west where the mountains of the Coastal Ranges prevent moist air from advancing far inland. The driest place is Death Valley in California, which has less than five centimetres of rain each year. It has also recorded North America's highest temperatures – up to 57°C. Under such conditions it is difficult for any form of life to survive. However, drought-resistant plants such as the creosote bush and saltbush have managed to grow in the desert. There are also many cacti, including the giant saguaro cactus which is found in Arizona and New Mexico.

The extreme temperatures and lack of water make it very difficult for animals to live in deserts. Most animals that do are reptiles and are nocturnal (active at night). They include many varieties of rattlesnakes and lizards.

The barren landscape of Death Valley (above) and (right) a rattlesnake

Prairies

Before the Great Plains of western America were cultivated, they were covered almost entirely by grassland or prairies. Very few trees were able to survive here because of the low rainfall and the frequent prairie fires. This climate provided an ideal environment for herds of grazing animals such as the American bison (buffalo) and the prongbuck. Once there were about 60 million bison on the prairies but by 1890, following excessive hunting, ranching and cereal farming, their numbers had fallen to about 300. Only small patches of prairie remain today. These are mainly found in park areas where the small remaining herds of bison can be protected.

The Everglades

The Everglades cover 10,500 square kilometres of southern Florida. Generally it is a vast waterlogged grassland, although along the coast there are dense mangrove forests. The Everglades National Park is a major tourist attraction. It is especially famous for its wildlife. Over 300 types of birds, including herons, spoonbills and ibises, live here alongside alligators, turtles and otters.

A herd of bison

Mangrove trees in the Everglades

Rivers and lakes

Rivers and lakes have played a major role in the development of the USA. For a long time they were the main routes used to explore the country. Today they are still an important means of transport and many cities have grown along their banks.

The Mississippi

The River Mississippi and its tributaries form the largest river system in North America. The Mississippi and its tributary the Missouri together form the third longest river in the world, with a total length of 5971 kilometres. The river flows southwards from Lake Itasca in Minnesota to the Gulf of Mexico, where it enters the sea.

The Mississippi has had a long history as a transport route. During the 19th century paddle steamers ploughed their way along its water. Today great chains of barges full of bulky raw materials are a common sight on the river.

The longest tributary of the Mississippi is the Missouri. The Missouri has eroded so much silt as it makes its way down from the Rockies and across the Great Plains that it is quite yellow in colour. It is sometimes called the 'big muddy'. The two rivers meet close to the city of St Louis.

As in many major rivers, the level of water in the Mississippi varies widely. In 1988 during a long drought the water was so low that barges ran aground on the sand banks in the river. In July 1993 heavy rain swelled the river 12 metres above its normal height. Even the spillways and raised banks built by engineers along the river could not hold back the water. A huge area of the Midwest was flooded as the river burst its banks, causing millions of dollars of damage.

The city of New Orleans has been built 90 kilometres from the point where the Mississippi reaches the sea. It is the second largest port in the United States.

Barges on the Mississippi at New Orleans

River Colorado

The Colorado River rises in the Rocky mountains. It is fed by melting snow before it flows southwest through the driest area of the USA and into the Gulf of California. Many dams have been built across it to store water in large reservoirs. These supply cities such as Los Angeles, Las Vegas and Phoenix with water. They are also used to generate hydro-electricity. Water from the river is also vital to farmers in the southwest who use it to irrigate their crops. So much water is taken out of the river that it almost vanishes before it reaches the sea.

The Grand Canyon in northwest Arizona is the most spectacular feature along the river. Each year more than three million people come to visit it. Most come just to view the scenery, but others enjoy white-water rafting along the river. You can also take a mule ride to the bottom of the canyon. It takes about five hours to go down but nine hours to climb back!

The Great Lakes

The five Great Lakes lie along the border between the USA and Canada. Lake Superior is the longest Great Lake, and the second largest lake in the world. The lakes are joined together by rivers which allow water to drain from one lake to the next. Water flowing from Lake Erie along the Niagara River eventually flows over the spectacular Niagara Falls before reaching Lake Ontario. The Great Lakes are linked to the sea by the St Lawrence Seaway, a system of canals. Ships carry cargoes of iron ore and coal to the many industrial cities on the shores of the lakes.

The River Colorado, deep in the Grand Canyon

Niagara Falls

Population

More than 250 million people live in the USA. Most Americans are descendants of people who migrated there from other parts of the world. This process began in the early 17th century when the British began to establish colonies on the Atlantic coast of North America. By 1776 the population was still less than three million. During the 19th century the pace of immigration from Europe increased so that by the beginning of the 20th century almost one million people a year were moving to the USA to seek a better life.

Outside the Stock Exchange in New York

Not all migrants were fortunate enough to have the choice of deciding whether or not they wished to live in North America. Most black Americans are descendants of slaves who were forcibly shipped to America to work on plantations and farms. Although slavery was eventually abolished during the Civil War in 1863, many black Americans had long been denied the privileges of American citizenship. Only since the rise of the Civil Rights Movement in the mid-20th century have black people been able to obtain better paid jobs, housing and education. Even today their average income is lower than that of white Americans and unemployment is much higher. But an increasing number of black Americans are gaining positions of economic and political influence. Some have become mayors of major cities.

Immigration into the United States continues today. Although 94 per cent of all Americans were born in the United States, people continue to enter the country both legally and illegally, particularly from Mexico, Puerto Rico and Cuba.

Native Americans
When the first Europeans landed on the mainland of the United States in 1513, about 1.5 million people were already living there. These native Americans were mistakenly called Indians by the

Europeans. They lived as separate tribes with no common language. Since 1831 native Americans have been forced to leave the land that they had occupied for thousands of years to live on reservations. These areas were usually where the land was of little value. Many thousands died from starvation or disease, or in wars fought against the American army. Even today most native Americans have to endure a poor standard of living on their reservations.

Population distribution

The population of the USA is very unevenly spread across the country. The most heavily populated areas are found in the northeast, especially along the Atlantic coastline or the shores of the Great Lakes, and in southern California along the coast from San Diego to San Francisco. These areas are heavily industrialised and are able to support a large urban population.

Elsewhere the population tends to be much more dispersed. High population densities can be found around the major cities of the interior but many people live either in small towns or on isolated farmsteads. Far fewer people live in the western half of the country. This is because the climate is too dry and the land is more mountainous.

Cooking maize on a Navajo Indian reserve

A ranch house in Colorado in winter

Farming

There are more than 2,300,000 farms in the USA, which produce a wide variety of food products. American farming is highly mechanised and it is estimated that an average farmer can produce enough food each year to feed 80 people.

Farming only accounts for three per cent of the labour force but many millions of other people are employed in food production or processing industries. Many farmers sell their products directly to food processing companies. In recent years farmers have been badly hit by over-production, which has caused prices to fall, and by high interest rates. Many small farmers have been forced to sell the land that their families have worked for generations.

Cereal production

America is the world's most important exporter of cereal grains. About three million tonnes of wheat are exported each year. The most important wheat-growing area is the Great Plains. This region stretches from Texas in the south, to North Dakota and across the border into Canada. Its gently sloping landscape is ideal for mechanised farming. Farms are very large and the wheat is sown in huge rectangular fields. In the south the wheat is sown in the autumn and harvested in early summer. This is known as winter wheat. Further north, the severe winters do not allow this and so wheat is sown in the spring.

Wheat farming in Montana

Driving cattle on a ranch

Cattle

The USA is the world's leading producer of beef. Millions of cattle are raised on the high plains to the west of the wheat belt where the climate is too dry to support crops. The ranches in this area are huge but the grazing is poor.

Beef cattle are also fattened in the corn belt which extends from Ohio in the east to Missouri and Minnesota in the west. The land is very fertile and there is enough rain to grow maize and soya beans. These crops are then used to fatten cattle and pigs. Dairy cattle are raised throughout the country and produce more than 65 million tonnes of dairy produce each year.

Agriculture in California

California is the most important agricultural state. It is best known for growing fruit and vegetables but cattle, milk, cotton and grapes are also important. Its warm climate gives it the advantage of a long growing season, which can last for ten months of each year. Most of the farms are very large, highly mechanised and tend to specialise in one or two crops. Irrigation is used to water crops during the dry summers. Costs are kept down by using low-paid labourers. These are often people who have migrated to California from Mexico.

California is the centre of the American wine industry. The best grapes are grown in the southern end of the Napa Valley. Here the vineyards climb from the valley floor on to the steep slopes of the surrounding mountains. Almost 200 wineries have been built in this area, making it one of the major wine-growing areas in the world.

Vines in the Napa Valley

Soil conservation

Farmers on the Great Plains are concerned that the wind does not blow away the soil. This happened during the 1930s when large parts of Texas, Oklahoma and Kansas became known as the Dust Bowl. Farmers try to protect the soil by planting long strips of different crops. These ripen at different times, which means that wide expanses of soil are not left exposed to the wind after harvesting.

Cities and their problems

During the 20th century there has been a rapid growth in the size of American cities. Today almost three quarters of the population live in towns or cities. Within most cities there are great differences between old and new, rich and poor. Most city centres have huge skyscrapers. Some old buildings have been preserved on their original sites but many more have been knocked down and replaced with office blocks, shopping centres, hotels or apartment buildings.

The growth of cities

The development of efficient public transport systems and the wide ownership of motor vehicles have allowed many Americans to move out of the overcrowded city centres to live in modern homes in the suburbs. The largest cities have spread out alarmingly. Industries, shopping centres and office blocks have also developed close to the edge of existing cities. This is because land is cheaper and traffic congestion is less severe.

In the northeast this process has resulted in an almost continuous built-up area stretching 800 kilometres from Boston to Washington. More than 60 million people live in this region, which contains more

Buildings old and new in San Fransisco

than 30 urban areas, including the cities of New York, Philadelphia and Baltimore. This huge concentration of people is sometimes called megalopolis. Other large built-up areas are developing between Chicago and Pittsburgh and in California between San Diego and San Francisco.

Inner city decline

One of the results of the growth of outer city areas (suburbs) has been the decline of the inner cities. Land in the centre of cities is very expensive. Many firms have found that they can no longer afford to stay and have moved out to new locations in the suburbs. As a result many people in the inner cities have lost their jobs. There are severe housing problems in most inner cities. In New York an estimated 90,000 people are homeless, many of whom are forced to sleep on the streets. Many others live in old buildings which are badly in need of repairs or improvements.

Most often it is the poorest people who live in the inner cities. In Philadelphia more than a quarter of the people of the inner city live below the poverty line.

Ethnic communities are often concentrated in their own neighbourhoods known as ghettos. The ghettos contain some of the worst examples of poverty in the United States. Recent figures suggest that a black child born in Harlem has a life expectancy of only 52 years, 20 years less than the average for the USA.

Rebuilding inner cities

People in many American cities have been unwilling to accept the decline of their inner cities and have started ambitious schemes to redevelop neglected areas. They are building new shopping centres, office blocks and leisure facilities in areas that were previously very run-down. Such schemes in their turn help to provide jobs.

One of the best examples of this redevelopment is the Inner Harbor area of Baltimore. The decaying wharves and warehouses have been knocked down. Modern office blocks, luxury hotels and carefully planned parks now stand in their place. Many of the old houses around the harbour have been renovated by young professional people who wish to live close to the city centre.

Harlem, a largely Black ghetto of New York

Redevelopment in Baltimore Inner Harbor

Major cities

Washington DC

Washington has been the capital of the USA since 1790. It stands on the northeast bank of the Potomac River in an area known as the District of Columbia, which is not part of any state.

The city has been carefully planned. It has wide tree-lined streets and many elegant buildings, parks and monuments. The most famous buildings are The White House, the home of the President, and the Capitol Building, in which Congress (see page 4) sits. No building is allowed to be more than 40 metres tall so that the Capitol can be seen from as far away as possible.

New York

New York is located at the point where the Hudson River flows into the Atlantic Ocean. Its natural harbour has enabled it to become one of the largest ports in the world. The entrance to the harbour is dominated by the famous Statue of Liberty (see title page). New York is the home of many buildings and institutions that are famous throughout the world. These include the United Nations building, the financial district of Wall Street (see page 14) and the entertainment area of Times Square and Broadway.

Capitol Building, Washington D.C.

Yellow cabs in Fifth Avenue, New York

New York has the largest population of all American cities. The city itself consists of five boroughs – Manhattan, Brooklyn, Queens, the Bronx and Staten Island – but the urban area has grown well beyond these limits. Manhattan, the focus of the city, is built on an island in the middle of the Hudson River. It is renowned for its impressive skyscraper skyline.

Chicago

Chicago is the third largest city in the USA and it is the most important industrial, commercial and financial centre of the Midwest. Its position has made it a very important focus of transport routes. O'Hare airport is the busiest in the world. Chicago is a major Great Lakes port and many of the continental rail and road routes are centred on the city. As a result it attracts more business conventions than any other city in the USA.

Chicago is also the birthplace of the skyscraper. A great fire in 1871 destroyed much of the city. When the city was re-built, steel-framed structures were used to support buildings up to 16 storeys high. Today these buildings are dwarfed by modern buildings such as the 100-storey John Hancock centre and the Sears Tower, which is 443 metres tall.

Los Angeles

The city of Los Angeles was founded by Spanish settlers in 1781 at the point where the Los Angeles river flowed across the narrow coastal plain between the San Gabriel mountains and the Pacific coast. Today the city has a population of more than 14 million people.

Los Angeles is probably best known as the centre of the film industry. The main movie studios are in Hollywood and the homes of many 'stars' are in the nearby residential district of Beverly Hills.

Los Angeles is also an important port and industrial centre. The main port area is in Long Beach. Its wide range of manufacturing industries include aerospace engineering, medical supplies, electronics and oil refining.

Perhaps more than any other city in the world Los Angeles is the city of the motor car. Its freeways have allowed the city to stretch over 100 kms along the Pacific coast. Car exhaust fumes have created a major air pollution problem (see page 26). So the city has passed laws forcing car owners to reduce exhaust gases from their cars. It is hoped that air quality will be 70 per cent cleaner by 2009.

Approaching Hollywood, in Los Angeles

Energy

The USA is the world's largest producer of nuclear energy and hydro-electricity. It is also the second largest producer of coal, oil and natural gas. However, even its vast resources cannot keep up with the enormous demand for energy in the United States.

Coal

The largest and oldest coal mining areas lie in the Appalachian coalfields, most notably in Pennsylvania, West Virginia and Kentucky. This coal has been mined for over a century and the remaining deposits have become increasingly expensive to

An open cast coal mine in Montana

exploit. The coal also tends to have a high sulphur content. When this type of coal is burnt it can increase environmental problems such as acid rain. So production

is gradually being switched to the vast deposits of the far west. In Wyoming and Montana the coal lies close to the surface and mechanical diggers can mine the coal at low cost. Although the coal is cheap to produce many people are concerned about the scars left on the landscape by this type of mining.

Oil and natural gas

The USA is not only the world's second largest producer of crude oil but it is also the largest importer. The rising price of oil has encouraged geologists to explore more remote parts of the United States in order

The Alaskan oil pipeline

to increase production. The richest oilfields lie along the Gulf Coast in Texas and Louisiana. Here the oil companies have built drilling platforms out at sea to recover oil that lies beneath the sea bed. Other important oil-producing states are California, Oklahoma and Alaska.

The Alaskan oilfield lies within the Arctic Circle at Prudhoe Bay. The sea in this area is frozen for much of the year. A pipeline 1300 kilometres long was built across Alaska to the port of Valdez so that oil tankers could transport the oil to the rest of the United States.

Hydro-electricity

The large rivers that flow through the mountainous regions of the USA provide ample opportunity for the production of hydro-electricity. In the western mountain region major rivers such as the Columbia and the Colorado have been dammed to produce electricity. The most famous project is the Tennessee Valley Authority, which was begun in 1933. Thirty-two dams were built on the River Tennessee and its tributaries. These dams produce vast amounts of electricity and also help to prevent flooding.

The Hoover Dam on the Colorado River

Nuclear energy

In 1957 the first nuclear power station in the USA was built at Shippingport in Pennyslvania. More than 75 other nuclear power stations have been built, making the United States the largest producer of nuclear power in the world.

It was hoped that nuclear power would provide a cheap form of electricity. But people who live near nuclear power stations are concerned that radioacitivity might be released into the atmosphere. This concern has increased since an accident occurred at Three Mile Island near Harrisburg in Pennsylvania. The Nuclear Regulatory Commission tries to ensure that power stations operate safely.

An anti-nuclear march

In March 1989 the oil tanker Exxon Valdez ran aground in Prince William Sound in southeast Alaska. It spilt more than ten million gallons of oil into the sea, much of which found its way on to the surrounding beaches. Many thousands of animals and birds, including sea otters and bald eagles were killed by the pollution. The Exxon Corporation has spent more than $1200 million (£800 million) trying to clean up the beaches and fishing grounds. Even so, scientists fear that it will take at least ten years for the fragile ecosystem to recover from the spill.

Manufacturing and trade

In almost every major town in the USA there are factories. The United States has the largest level of industrial production in the world and employs more than 20 million people. The most important industries are motor vehicles, aeroplanes, food products, chemicals, machinery and electrical goods.

The industrial northeast

The most important industrial region of the USA is the northeast. This region lies between Boston and Baltimore in the east and Kansas and Minneapolis in the west. It contains a full range of manufacturing industries. Much of its success has been due to the ability of the population to invent new and successful products.

The cities on the shores of the Great Lakes and western Pennsylvania have long been important for heavy industries such as steelmaking. The steel industry was based on supplies of coal from Pennsylvania and iron ore from Minnesota. These raw materials could be shipped across the Great Lakes or along major rivers and canals to the steelworks in cities such as Pittsburgh, Cleveland and Buffalo. Other lakeside cities were able to use the steel to create other products. Detroit, for example, is the headquarters of major motor vehicle producers such as Ford and General Motors.

For many years, factories in the Great Lakes region have been closing down. It has sometimes been called the Rust Belt as

Scrap metal is recycled at a steelworks in Ohio.

factories are closed down and the land is left derelict. There are many reasons why this has happened. Modern plastics, for example, are replacing steel for some products. Labour in some other parts of the United States is cheaper. Those factories that remain have become increasingly automated, so many local people have lost their jobs.

Robots at work on a car assembly line in Detroit

Industrial growth in the south

The fastest-growing industrial regions of the USA are the south and southwest. This area has a warmer climate than the old industrial regions of the northeast. There is less congestion and plenty of land available on which to build modern factories. Wages for workers also tend to be lower than in the northern states. California is now the most important manufacturing state in America. It is particularly well known for its computer and micro-electronics industries, which are well established to the south of San Francisco. This area has become known as Silicon Valley.

Silicon Valley in California

Trade

The USA is the world's greatest trading nation. The value of the goods and services produced in the United States is far greater than in any other country. Its main exports are machinery, transport equipment, chemicals and foodstuffs. Its main trade partners are Canada, Japan and the countries of the European Community.

The Americans also consume more goods than any other country. Since 1976 the USA has experienced a trade deficit. This means that it imports more goods than it sells abroad. Some of this deficit is caused by the huge amounts of fuel and raw materials that are used by American industries. In recent years, however, there has been great concern in the United States that it is importing more manufactured goods than it exports. Japanese goods have been especially successful at finding markets within the USA. This has meant that many American firms have been unable to make a profit and have been forced to shut down. Many people would like to restrict imports from other countries, especially Japan.

Transport

Roads

There are about 143 million cars in the USA and more than 6,360,000 kilometres of roads. Americans use cars for most of the journeys that they make, even the very short ones.

The road system includes more than 88,000 kilometres of interstate highways. This is a network of multiple lane expressways stretching across the whole country. In fact, you can drive from the east coast to the west coast without seeing a single traffic light! These highways are widely used by trucks, which carry about 25 per cent of all the freight transported in the United States.

Trucks transport a quarter of all freight in the USA.

Car-sharing (left) helps to avoid congestion on freeways (above: Los Angeles).

One unwanted side effect of the volume of traffic in American cities is air pollution. The city of Los Angeles, for example, is frequently covered by a brown cloud of smog during the summer. The main pollutant in this cloud is ozone. This is formed when sunlight reacts with the exhaust fumes from cars. It can cause sore throats, headaches and breathing problems, and many young children suffer with asthma.

Railways

The United States railway network is the second largest in the world after Russia. It has over 270,000 kilometres of railway track, most of which is only used for freight. The railways are used for transporting bulky materials such as coal, grain, chemicals and motor vehicles. About 35 per cent of all freight traffic in the USA is handled by rail. Some trains are over a kilometre long.

A third of freight is carried by rail.

Only one per cent of people travelling between cities use the railways. This is because it takes much longer to travel by rail than by air. The railway journey between New York and Los Angeles takes about 60 hours, but only 6 hours by air.

The inter-city passenger network is run by Amtrak. They encourage passengers to travel on the railways for pleasure. Long distance trains have special carriages called dome cars which give an unrestricted view of the landscape. The timetable is arranged so that the most picturesque parts of the routes can be viewed in daylight. The Amtrak network includes some of the greatest railway journeys in the world. The Desert Wind, for example, takes two days to travel the 3800 kilometres between Los Angeles and Chicago. It crosses the deserts of Utah and California and passes through the spectacular Rocky Mountains and across the Great Plains.

Many large American cities also have network of electrical railways which bring millions of people to work each day. Systems such as the New York subway and the Bay Area rapid transit system in San Franciso help to ease traffic congestion in the city centre during the rush hour.

Air travel
Air travel is very important because of the very large size of the country. It allows passengers to travel long distances in a short time. There are more than 15,400 airfields in operation. Most are small, privately owned airfields which handle only a small number of internal flights each day. The largest airports handle millions of passengers each year and thousands of flights each day. Four of the five busiest airports in the world are located within the United States at Chicago, Atlanta, Los Angeles and Dallas/Fort Worth.

Dallas Fort Worth Airport

Life and leisure

Most Americans enjoy one of the richest lifestyles in the world. Most homes are equipped with a television, telephone, refrigerator and many labour-saving devices.

Education

American children have to attend school between seven and 16 years of age but most begin when they are five or six years old.

Exam time at Harvard University

They complete 12 years or grades before they finish high school. Between 85 and 90 per cent of children attend public schools which are paid for by local taxes. American high schools are often very large and offer a broad range of subjects. Most schools are very well equipped, although this is not the case in many inner cities or poorer areas.

Many pupils choose to continue their education at college or university. University courses normally last for four years, whereas community college courses last two years. Attending college can be very expensive. Most students have to take out loans to cover the cost of their education.

Shopping

The main shopping areas are no longer located in the centre of major cities but are found in huge shopping centres in the suburbs. These contain a wide variety of department stores and specialist shops which can cater for almost every need. They are usually built close to major roads and are surrounded by huge car parks.

A shopping mall in Minneapolis

Although the importance of the city centre as a shopping area has declined, large cities such as New York still have some of the best known stores in the world. Macy's advertises itself as the world's largest store, whilst Bloomingdales caters for customers who can afford more expensive tastes.

Leisure

The most popular national pastime is watching television, but more and more people are finding other ways to enjoy their recreation time. At state fairs attractions include rodeo displays, concerts, and fairground entertainments. Local festivals are also popular. The best know of these is Mardi Gras, held each year in New Orleans. This includes a great carnival in which decorated floats parade through the city.

Theme parks are also hugely popular throughout the United States. Disney World and the Epcot centre in Florida attract more than 20 million visitors a year. Most theme parks are based around one idea, but this complex offers an incredible variety of things to do, such as fantasy space rides, jungle cruises, steamboat trips or visiting a wild west cowboy town.

Sports

Most Americans enjoy some form of sport, either playing or watching on a regular basis. Swimming, cycling and jogging are the most popular activities but baseball, American football and basketball are the most popular spectator sports. These attract large crowds and huge television audiences.

American athletes have a great record of success in international competition. They have won more gold medals at the Olympic Games than any other country. In 1996 the city of Atlanta will host the Olympic Games.

Cinderella's Castle, in Disney World, Florida

A game of basketball

The USA in the world

In its relatively short history the USA has emerged as probably the most powerful country in the world. It has the world's largest economy and plays a leading role in international politics.

The United States was a founder member of the United Nations, which has its headquarters in New York. It was formed in 1945 to promote peace and co-operation between nations. The United States is a permanent member of the Security Council which tries to keep the peace between countries involved in disputes. It has sent its troops to many troubled parts of the world to try to keep the peace.

The United Nations building, New York

The United States has also played a leading role in a number of other international organisations. These include the North Atlantic Treaty Organisation (NATO), in which all members have agreed to come to the aid of each other if they are attacked by another country. It also is a member of the Organisation of American States (OAS) which encourages member countries to support each other, and the Organisation for Economic Cooperation and Development (OECD), which tries to determine economic policies for the western world.

Finance
The fortunes of the economy of the USA are of worldwide importance. Many of the world's most important companies are American and their products are well known throughout the world. Wall Street in New York is the most important financial centre in the world. Any change in share prices on the New York Stock Exchange has a strong influence on economic prospects throughout the world.

The arts
Americans have made a huge impact in the arts especially during the 20th century. The work of authors such as John Steinbeck, Ernest Hemmingway, Harper Lee and Alice Walker has been translated

into many languages and read around the world. Artists such as Jackson Pollock, Andy Warhol and Richard Estes have gained worldwide recognition for their work.

The USA has also become the home of many priceless collections of art. The John Paul Getty Museum in California, the Art Institute of Chicago and the Museum of Modern Art in New York house some of the greatest collections in the world. The Lincoln Centre in New York is one of the most important venues in the world, housing the Metropolitan Opera House and the New York State Theatre. The New York Philharmonic and the Chicago Symphony are amongst the most accomplished orchestras in the world.

Americans have also taken the lead in many areas of popular entertainment. Jazz, blues and rock music all originated in the United States. Musicals originally performed on Broadway have reached a worldwide audience. Hollywood is the centre of the world's film industry and the Oscars presented each year at the Academy Awards ceremony are considered the highest honour in the movie industry.

Space exploration

The Kennedy Space Centre at Cape Canaveral in Florida has been the launch pad for America's exploration of Space. Alan Shepherd became the first American in Space in 1961. On July 20th 1969, Neil Armstrong became the first person to set foot on the Moon. The Space shuttle has allowed astronauts to complete ever more difficult missions such as the repair of the Hubble telescope in Space in 1993.

Street musicians in New Orleans, Louisiana

A Space shuttle is launched.

Index and summary

Population	250,372,000
Area	9,372,571 square kilometres
Capital city	Washington DC
Major cities	New York, Los Angeles, Chicago, Atlanta, Dallas, Detroit, Houston, Philadelphia, San Francisco
Main exports	Machinery, transport equipment and motor vehicles, chemicals, foodstuffs
Main imports	Machinery, motor vehicles, clothing, metals, crude and partly refined petroleum
Longest river	Mississippi-Missouri 5,971 kilometres
Highest peak	Mt McKinley 6194 metres
Lowest point	Death Valley, California, 86 metres below sea level
Currency	100 cents to 1 dollar $
Religion	Christian, but all religions are practised
Language	English
Life expectancy	73 years (male), 80 years (female)